HER VOICE
Matters

Inspiring Women to Share Their Stories

Evangelist Joan Evans DaCosta

HER VOICE MATTERS. Copyright © 2024. Joan Evans DaCosta. All Rights Reserved.

Printed in the United States of America.

No portion of this book may be reproduced, stored in a retrieval system, or transmitted in any form or by any means, except for brief quotations in printed reviews, without the prior written permission of DayeLight Publishers or Joan Evans DaCosta.

ISBN: 978-1-958443-88-0 (paperback)

Unless otherwise stated, Scripture quotations are taken from the New King James Version. Copyright © 1982 by Thomas Nelson, Inc. Used by permission. All rights reserved. Bible text from the New King James Version® is not to be reproduced in copies or otherwise by any means except as permitted in writing by Thomas Nelson, Inc., Attn: Bible Rights and Permissions, P.O. Box 141000, Nashville, TN 37214-1000.

Scripture quotations marked (NIV) are taken from the Holy Bible, New International Version®, NIV®. Copyright © 1973, 1978, 1984 by Biblica, Inc.™ Used by permission of Zondervan. All rights reserved worldwide.

There's no substitute for obedience.
Our generation is heavily defiled.
(Hebrews 10:22; Colossians 2:14)
Every satisfaction comes with obedience. We are in a generation where evil and abuse are evident. Several of our girls and women are defiled. I am declaring that there's no need to walk in condemnation anymore. I pray that the good Lord will fortify your soul with the joy that brings that unconditional love, peace, and forgiveness.

Real Life Stories
Transforming Women's Lives for Greatness.
Women who are experiencing low self-esteem and bitterness.
Women who are hurting resulting in hopelessness and brokenness.
Women from Christian backgrounds who lack the necessary biblical tools to overcome these challenges.

The MacArthur Study Bible ESV was the first gift given to me by Mr. Elon DaCosta thirteen years before I gave him my hands in marriage.

Other inspiration arose by spending quality time with the Holy Spirit and engaging with Sister Sister Conferences in different parts of Jamaica. My critical thinking skills, as well as a collection of thoughts, feelings, and experiences, comprise this book.

According to the Word of God, we should not lean on our own understanding but in all our ways, acknowledge the Lord and He will direct our path (see Proverbs 3:5-6). Whatever gift the Holy Spirit has granted me is not for my personal benefit but for building up the body of Christ; to give comfort, information, exhortation and edification that will benefit those of faith and those who have strayed in a positive and meaningful way. If you believe, you will receive.

that the God of our Lord Jesus Christ, the Father of glory, may give to you the spirit of wisdom and revelation in the knowledge of Him, (Ephesians 1:17 – NKJV).

ACKNOWLEDGMENTS

A special thank you to my children Shornel, Taniel, Shevel, who played a significant role in my boldness and strength. They always reminded me, "Mom, prayer is more powerful than the problems. Come, let us pray." "Mom, please stay safe and be positive." Children are a heritage of God's kingdom.

Thanks to my husband, Elon A. DaCosta, for loving and accepting me for who I am.

Thanks to Minister Carmen Swack Menzies, my mentor and Rev. Marsha Daniels Powell, my motivator at Bible College.

Thanks to my medical doctors and surgeon for their love and support. They were chosen and appointed by God for such a time as this.

To Minister Claude Jarrett, the man behind the cameras for my YouTube Ministry "Evangelism Eye Watch" (EEW). He has been with me since its inception in 2020.

Thanks to all the pastors, leaders, and members at the International Worship Centre and Faith Ministries who stood by me.

AFFIRMATION

This book came about from a vision from the Lord in 2020. Habakkuk 2:2 reminded me to write the vision. It is my prayer that this book, which was influenced, directed, and appointed by the Holy Spirit, will open the eyes of the readers to what God says about women.

Women are exceptional, and we are given the right to live happily and enjoy it to the fullest from an infant, child, adolescent, young lady, and motherhood. This is why it is important to protect their wellbeing both physically and psychologically. We must represent the intrinsic morals and values of Godly nature.

We are also given the right to be called heirs of God's promises. Proverbs 31 declares the transfiguration of a woman who is wise in her ways as well as her words, work, and conduct—a virtuous woman.

Then the Lord answered me and said, "Write the vision and engrave it plainly on [clay] tablets so that the one who reads it will run." (Habakkuk 2:2 – AMP).

A vision that is plain will energize and ignite the fire of God in everyone who comes in contact with it. It is also important that we understand the purpose that God has for our lives.

I distanced myself from self-doubt and negativity. I am renewed in my mind daily; my faith is stronger than ever before. I put on the whole armour of God. I am daily loaded. I am not concerned with the negative opinions of people. I am fearfully and wonderfully made.

I gave all diligence to write to you about the common salvation and exhort you to contend for the faith and do not grow weary in well doing, for no one who put their trust in the Lord will be desolate.

Let me remind you this day that the Lord is a refuge for all who are oppressed, and He is a refuge in times of trouble.

FOREWORD

This book is a most timely and valuable resource. It is a timely book as it exposes the writer's vulnerability yet shows that in all trials and challenges, God remains her anchor, her solid rock on which she continues to stand.

Writing is the most demanding form of thinking that reveals matters of the heart. When we write down our own experiences, pain, and journey, it helps to strengthen the fortitude of others who just might be facing their line in the sand.

Your method of coping and survival can be the help, guide, comfort, or direction to others. Some of us can live such a superficial life, but when others can read and realize they are not alone and that challenges come to make or break you, then you can truly rejoice, knowing that God is forever a present help in times of trouble.

Since God shows no favouritism, what He has done for Joan, He will surely do the same for each one of us. We thank her for this insightful and encouraging account of her life.

This book is indeed a labour of love. The writer's passion demonstrates a strong desire to aid other women in finding their own identity in a world that can be so callous and cold. Joan's test has become her testimony and will be so for many generations to come. Having once been enslaved by pain in her earlier years, she has experienced liberation where she is no longer bound. She is no longer held captive by the kingdom of darkness. She is now a witness of the kingdom of God, where she has been transformed into a daughter of light.

So, we will rejoice for reading this book, for Jehovah God must get His glory. Amen.

Wynsomme Lewin
Minister of the Gospel
International Worship Centre and Faith Ministries
Montego Bay

TABLE OF CONTENTS

Acknowledgments vii
Affirmation ix
Foreword xi
Introduction 15
Chapter 1: The Challenges That Women Face 17
Chapter 2: Coping With Single Life And Temptations As A Female Christian 37
Chapter 3: There Is A Purpose In Every Test 45
Chapter 4: Prayers Changed My Life When Uncertainty Set In 57
Chapter 5: What the Bible Says About Domestic Violence Against Your Spouse 75
Chapter 6: Discovering Your Identity Behind The Mask 87
Chapter 7: A Virtuous Black Woman 91
Chapter 8: God Is Not Finish With You Yet 95
About The Author 103

INTRODUCTION

I am a living testimony of the challenges of life. This book will transform the lives of our women for greatness. I will deliver God's natural words. This book will also highlight some key moments in my life.

True diversity is having the ability to open up your mind to all opinions from all women, understanding that we are women created by God with unique abilities.

As you read this book, it will help you to help others on their journey with sickness, divorce, death of a spouse, abuse, marital problems, the spirit of seduction and shame, rejection, harassment at work, provocation, poverty, obsession, perversion, unforgiveness, abortion, miscarriage, barrenness, brokenness, murder, and loneliness.

I implore you to get involved and maintain a loving attitude, which involves your mind, soul, spirit, and body. The mind is a battlefield. Do not conform to what the devil is telling you about your past, but be transformed by the renewing of your mind.

Character is never built on your status in life. It is built on the circumstances of life. Your entrance into this world system does not define your existence. According to the Word of God in Jeremiah 29:11, God knew you before you were formed in the womb of your mother; He knows the plans He has for your life. It is a plan to give you good health and prosper you in all your ways. God is not a man that He should lie (see Number 23:19). If He said He is going to do it, He will do it. Your circumstances must change lives.

God told Jacob that his name was no longer Jacob but Israel. Paul told Timothy that the purpose of his teaching was to develop character in those he taught. In essence, our God-given purpose is embedded in our DNA by the Creator Himself.

CHAPTER 1

THE CHALLENGES THAT WOMEN FACE

My life is a living testimony of the challenges women face from childhood and adolescence into motherhood. It took courage, confidence, commitment, and a critical period to overcome these hurdles.

I know it is hard to love some women when we think of the pain they cause us in our relationships and ordinary lives. Most of the time, in our fallen state, we tend to speak and think foolishly. However, John 13:35 reiterates that fellowship happens when mercy wins over hate. Fellowship is a place of grace and forgiveness. Some simple women we take for granted are carriers of living water. They exhibit sweet souls and great companionships.

It is impossible to fellowship without forgiveness. Bitterness, unforgiveness, and resentment always destroy fellowship, especially when it is intentional.

Don't be afraid to share your testimony. Don't be afraid to share what God intended to use in you. Faith possesses life. After you have read this book, your chains must be broken, yokes must be shattered, burdens must be lifted and you must emerge in divine purpose with strength and peace that surpasses human comprehension. Love must be the primary key to a life of transformation.

The story of my life unfolds. The world was an endless cave, and I was alone and lost. I was as lonely as the sea on a stormy night. My heart could hold no more, and I wept as I ran towards the grey board and concrete house.

In German Town—Maroon Town, Saint James, a small community bordering the parish of Saint Elizabeth, I grew up with my dear, sweet grandmother. Oliver Lena Evans was a wonderful, faithful, and prayerful wife, and my grandfather, Lionel Gaddy Evans, was a pioneer in farming and family values. He departed this life in 1979 with his hands in my lap. My most frequently visited places were church on a Sunday morning and Sunday School in the evenings at my grandparent's home. I never experienced hardship or abuse around my grandparents; they were extraordinary parents.

On the morning of October 20th, 1980, at about 6 am, I woke up to the cool autumn breeze and the sweet-smelling aroma of chocolate tea with roasted breadfruit. I walked towards the back door of the six-apartment board house and stretched my thin, tall legs. I saw my grandma inside the outdoor wooden-structure kitchen preparing breakfast for us. I said, "Good morning, grandma."

She looked up and replied in a very low-pitched sound, "My child, go get ready for school."

I moved towards the bathroom door like a snail curling up in its shell. I could tell and feel that something was about to happen, and it would be horrifying because my entire body was motionless. The feeling of despair ripped my heart like a mighty rushing wind.

As the hours passed, I could hear my grandma calling out to me, "Sher! Come to me." I struggled with the sad and fearful feeling inside until I reached the kitchen and finally ate my breakfast. Now it was time for me to leave for school. I could hardly say goodbye to her, but I glanced at her and saw when she took up some gravel from the ground and threw them at me jokingly. During this time, she uttered, "Hurry up and go to school. You might not come home and see me." At that moment, right on the spot, I felt the earth move from under my feet; my entire body shivered, and there was a horrific sting and feeling like the last drop of blood in my body clotted to the ground.

I managed to reach school, and throughout that entire day, the skies were overcast, and so were my features. Later in the day, while I was seated in my classroom, my teacher broke the news of the death of my grandmother to me.

My entire life was shattered. I dashed from the classroom and just kept running as if I had no intention of stopping. I finally came to a halt when I realized a gully was before me. I tucked my body between four banana trees for several hours. I was speechless; dark clouds were hanging everywhere. My tears were like banana stains when I wiped my eyes. My feet where blistered and numb; my mind was working like a numbskull person, wondering what to do next.

I heard voices; I heard steps, but I could not speak. Night had fallen, and only the light from flying insects could be seen flying around. I felt the presence of someone lift me from the dark, but I could not see who it was. I found myself sitting in a chair at my grandma's home, crying. I wept until the day of her burial. No one could take the place of sweet grandma, the one who bore the sweetest name. No wonder the composer rightly stated, "Life won't be the same without the sugar cane." Life has never been the same for me. I went through so many transformations.

Life for me was an unsolved puzzle. The questions I remember hearing from everyone were related to Grandma's strict instructions about who in the family should take proper guardianship of me. Years went by, and I was still at my grandparents' home with other family members when my dad and his young spouse moved in. I had some pretty rough times after my other siblings were born. My stepmother did not show me much love; her love towards me was different, even though I was a loving and respectful child. I remember hearing her say when she thought she had scolded me sufficiently, "You can soon be on your own. All you need is three firesticks and two brick stones to become a full woman." Words like 'idiot' were often used to describe me, and these words hit me hard. I would often question myself: What does she really mean? Does she have good or bad intentions? What would follow was a severe beating from my dad, which was unexplainable. Life was very challenging. I began working part-time and attending school from an early age. During this time, I learned to take dental impressions for people who needed dentures. I am not at liberty to mention names.

Things began spiralling out of control. I observed that the manager of the firm was a pervert, based on his conversations. His inappropriate touches became unbearable, and I was afraid of his hollow cheeks, receding forehead, arched nose, and the creepy sound of his footsteps and suspicious movements. One day, I left the office and never returned.

Years went by, and the daily challenges and mounting pressures led to a division in my home due to a broken relationship between my dad and his spouse. Most of the time, I was on my own, though family members lived nearby. I knew my father loved me deeply, but somewhere along the way, his entire mental state deteriorated, even to the point where he started smoking whatever he could find. My father was only home on weekends, as he worked away from home.

I vividly remember being molested by an older boy while I was home alone. I was robbed of my innocence.

My school average of an "A" plummeted because my mental stability was shattered. I was extremely scared. I was not a talkative child and was mostly timid.

I was very fearful of men, to the point where I thought I would never have a relationship in my life. I would shake like a leaf whenever they came around. The harsh reality of life continued to plague my development. I ran away from home after school one day in my uniform and went to live with an aunt. Not long afterward, her husband joined us, and that was where my real nightmare began—the old Jamaican saying, "jump out of the frying pan and into the fire," described my situation perfectly. I suffered in silence and misery due to her husband's frequent sexual advances. I was terrified of what would happen if I exposed this predator, as he was the main breadwinner of the household. It took immense courage to stand up to this abuse. Only God knows the pain and suffering I endured; I did not wear my wounds on the outside. I could not focus on my schoolwork. To escape this harassment, I sought the friendship of a neighboring family with children my age. They helped me with schoolwork, but this did not go down well. I was accused of bringing a man into the house and was thrown out and barred from school—the principal was their friend.

During the troubled years of my teenage life, my grandmother's instructions were forgotten by both my guardians, but not by God. My friends' families tried to get me back into school, but it was unsuccessful. I was now vulnerable, burdened, and alone in a dark world controlled by various desires. The accusations were painful; the treatment was onerous. I remember her voice telling me to leave the house, reminding me that I had no mother or anywhere to live. Some people even believed that I did not have a mother based on the image that was painted. Frankly, I began to think I was adopted, as the most frequent story I heard was, "Remember, you don't have a mother." Not long after, I inadvertently took the wrong path and became a teenage mother with a baby boy.

My dreams and aspirations seemed shattered. But there was always a calm, inner voice telling me that He was not finished with me yet. I faced real struggles, and eventually, I found my mother, though there wasn't much she could do to help me at that time. I had to take live-in jobs just to have shelter and care. On one occasion, while working as a household helper, the husband of the house attempted to have an affair with me. This was a fierce battle, and I fought with all my might. By God's mercy, I was spared. I immediately boarded a country bus and returned to my roots. It wasn't long before I took on another live-in job to survive. These jobs were not easy for a young girl, and there were days I would break down from the hard work. I knew God had a plan for my life, and His purpose could not be aborted.

I never stopped striving. I was always employed. One day, I felt the urge to visit my aunt, so I made my way to her home in the country, where we had a long talk. I told her that I wanted to join the police force, but since I had been expelled from school, she would need to get my credentials from the principal and give me the go-ahead.

This was a courageous and critical moment for me. She responded, "All that I've done to you was in the name of love. Love is hard when parents want good for their children. If you see it as hate, mi nuh hate you." I forgave her because what she displayed was obsession and ignorance, masked as good parenting.

Today, I am thankful that mercy rewrote my life, and I am no longer a slave to pain. I now share a great relationship with my mother and siblings and never miss a family reunion. My dad gave his life to the Lord before he passed away. I am happy to say I was able to pray with him and give him the necessary care before his departure.

The lessons from my childhood, adolescence, and motherhood experiences taught me that life and death are in the power of the tongue. Therefore, I am obligated to speak only what God wants me to speak. No man can shut the doors God has opened in your life. We must surround ourselves with people who have our best interests at heart. Never become vulnerable with those who do not have your best interest at heart. Do not worry about anything when God has full control over your life. In this life, when people reject and resent you, let them go. By your words and actions, you are justified, and by your actions and words, you are condemned. Nothing in this life is greater than a relationship with God.

Good parenting for my life seemed to have died after the death of my grandparents. Expectations, dreams, and visions were a part of my background, even in the midst of my adversities. Nonetheless, adversities sometimes serve as the agent of change. Agent of change can be either good or bad, joy or sadness; this can attract feelings of disappointment or accomplishment.

The truth is, I never, for one moment, regretted my struggles because they became my testimony. A problem shared is a problem solved. My advice to parents and those who desire to become parents: words are powerful. All words have the potential power to disturb the chemical balance of the brain cells. The power of words can destroy everything you are hoping for; words have the ability to build you or break you. They have a significant impact on children and can be as addictive as drugs. Words are the platform for both development and underdevelopment. Words carry verdicts, so we must carefully model our choice of words when communicating with children during their stages of life.

Women in Warfare

Women are designed for greatness, so let me remind you of some great women who had their fair share of challenges in the Bible.

Shiphrah and Puah were midwives, but they stood their ground irrespective of Pharoah's order, and in the end, they were rewarded by God (see Exodus 1).

It was Mary who reminded us that all power belongs to God (see Luke 1:46).

Ruth's commitment, dedication, love, and longsuffering, bearing the burden of others through trying times, made her and Noami both victorious. Their steadfast loyalty was impeccable (see Ruth 1:16).

Esther affirmed, "If I perish I perish but I am going to see the king" with courage, confidence, and commitment in a critical moment as a young Jewish girl. She risked her life in the king's house to save the Jewish people from the wrath of destruction (see Esther 4:16).

It was Rehab who reminded us to never give up on anyone, no matter what may come our way or how deep in sin we have gone (see Hebrews 11:3).

The woman with the issue of blood reminds us that God is still God, and He has not changed (see Mark 5:25-33). Seek him first and His righteousness and all healing and miracles will be granted to us (see Matthew 6:33), according to His will and purpose. God is still in the healing business. When all fails, seek Jesus.

The woman of Samaria reminds us that she was transformed from the dominion of darkness into the kingdom of light. She faced struggles and challenges in finding her identity as an outcast. She had an encounter with Jesus—the one who showed her unconditional love (see John 4:5-30).

I know that every greatness begins with a powerful thought. Always remember that your challenges will not stifle your aspirations. You have the tenacity, willpower, and patience to overrule and subdue the wicked force of darkness from over your life. Jesus is never frantic or anxious about any situation. He is not driven by emotions. He is guided by the Father, and the more you commune with God, the more you become immune to fear, worry, and anxiety. God's Word stands true forever, and He understands our pain. God is the strength of every situation, and He said He will never leave us nor forsake us. No one who puts their trust in God will be desolate (see Psalm 34:22). If you serve the Lord, God, the Father, will bless you. Trust God and reach out to Him.

The Lord will fight for us. He gives power to the weak, and to those who have no might, He increases their strength. If you wait upon the Lord, you will surely be rewarded. When things are not going your way, don't get frustrated; trust in God's way because God sees what we cannot see.

My Journey Continues

I pray for your faith that you will walk according to God's purpose and promise for your life.

For many years, my life was a shipwreck. I was struggling to find the right road to choose. With so many trials and temptations and no strong support, I would always seek love from a man to fulfil that void, but that never ended well. It is important to speak up early and get the help that is necessary. Don't hide your pain or the problems will spill over into your everyday life. I was always passionate about God, but back then, I was looking in and looking out. I had so many convictions and encounters with the Lord throughout my years of living on earth. The truth is, I was fixing my life the way I believed it was supposed to be fixed, not knowing or having a clue about God's Word. I was so busy with the pleasures of sin.

In 2001, I decided to give Jesus a try. I went searching for a church and found a kingdom where I felt the peace of God. That kingdom transformed my life richly in the wisdom and knowledge of God. I properly aligned my antenna to connect with the kingdom frequency. I surrendered my life to Christ and got baptized on April 29th, 2001. God knows this was when the real struggles of life began. I got knocked down but not destroyed. I struggled along the way.

The pressure of a toxic work environment where I was sabotaged at the highest level and a tough working condition and demanding tasks brought me to a point in my life where I didn't want to go to work anymore. I felt like quitting prematurely, but something got a hold on me. Like the woman with the issue of blood who kept pressing into that crowd, I kept moving over those hurdles for years.

God did not say that the road would be easy. Often I remembered that it was no mistake when God gave me my present career. I had been serving gracefully for over thirty-three years; I did it according to **Colossians 3:23.** I sat my first exam and came out with a mark of 64.8%, which was a failed result. The elevation process was not easy for me. It took me twenty-one years before I was promoted to the first bar. This was not a gift but an exam mark of 79% in my senior years, sitting with all the young, bright future men and women. It was courage, confidence, and commitment that brought me through.

Then came that critical moment when I decided I would not sit any more exams. I can vividly remember my children saying to me, "Go, Mom. Whatever you do will help to motivate us in school too." I started praying, when suddenly the Word of God came to me from Psalm 75:6, "For promotion cometh neither from the east, nor from the south. But God." (NIV), He is the Judge. He putteth down one, and setteth up another (see Psalm 75:7). God alone determines where favour rest with you. God will break you to position, promote, and put you in the right place at the right time. David's patience worked in his favour. His patience allowed God to promote him at the right time and in the right place.

Whosoever is born of God overcomes the world, but for anyone who fears the Lord, the Son of God will arise with healing in His wings (see Malachi 4:2). How can anyone keep the affairs of the heart pure? By guarding it with the Word of God (see Psalms 119:9-

11). The Lord will give you grace to make your way pure and give you your heart's desire.

The worst has passed, and the best is yet to come. A woman who has been crushed for purpose faces many and varied setbacks, trials and tribulations, demotions, character assassination, lies, plots, and deceptions; survived surgical proceedings, including breast issues, are among the most common ones—but God. Purpose cannot die, and if you are feeling rejected, busted, and disgusted about your past, it is not over. I have news for you: it is not over until God says it is over.

I have decided that the enemy will not make me a bad example. Giving up is not an option. You will have tribulations, but don't quit. I realised the purpose for which I came; hence, I am aligned with what God wants to deposit into my life. I am not programmed into this world system anymore. I am intentional about my spiritual life. I am no longer the subject of demotion, an outcast, or a casualty of procrastination.

Ways to Address the Heavens

Humility and Gratitude

This is the ability to recognize our strengths, heights, and depths with honesty and grace.

Oh, that men would give thanks to the Lord for His goodness, and for His wonderful works to the children of men! (Psalm 107:21).

To make known to the sons of men His mighty acts, and the glorious majesty of His kingdom. (Psalm 145:12).

The Lord is faithful in all He promises. His rulership endures through all generations.

My flesh and my heart fail; but God is the strength of my heart and my portion forever. (Psalm 73:26).

The Lord will bless those who are humble (see Isaiah 66:2). God is working it out all for your good; something good is coming to you. You may ask, "Can any good thing come out of Nazareth?" Oh, yes. Something good is coming to you. When people flaunt about themselves, it doesn't really matter. But when the Lord commends someone, it makes a difference.

God works in ways we may not know, and we cannot tell. Paul says the person who flaunts should only do so because of the abundance of God's grace (see 2 Corinthians 10:17-18). Every assault of oppression and stagnation against your life is terminated now.

For the Word of God is active and alive right now, and it is sharper than any two-edged sword (see Hebrews 4:12). God wants to raise your standard of living. God wants to finish what He started within you. For He that began a good work will continue to the end (see Philippians 1:6).

God is faithful, and He will make a way where there seems to be no way. For with God, nothing is impossible (see Luke 1:37).

Beloved, do not think it strange concerning the fiery trial which is to try you, as though some strange thing happened to you; but rejoice to the extent that you partake of Christ's sufferings, that when His glory is revealed, you may also be glad with exceeding joy. (1 Peter 4:12-13).

Many are the affliction of the righteous, but the Lord delivers them out of them all (see Psalm 34:19).

From Bitter to Better

- God heard your prayers and knows everything the enemy has done to you. You will recover it all.
- God says you are to forgive anyone who does you harm or wrong, just as Christ has forgiven you.
- Bitterness is wrong. It can kill you; just as Delilah vexed Sampson to his death (see Judges 16:16).
- The devil cannot keep you down. There are many dream-killers in this world system, but the Lord is a way-maker.
- You are overcoming your adversity to inspire hope. Your mouth is a major part of your transformation. Speak love. Speak what you want to always remember as positive. People will treat you according to how you treat yourself. Therefore, as you begin to accept the beauty God has placed inside you, others will begin to appreciate you more.
- The Word of God confessed will begin to transform you into the original image God designed you to be. Being a child of God is a lifestyle. It takes confidence, courage, commitment, and critical thinking.
- God will perfect the things concerning your life. Did you know that faith gives substance and hope to every bittersweet moment in your life? Yes, it does indeed; this is a biblical principle. Faith is what builds your confidence, courage, and commitment, and helps you through critical periods. I have lived every phase of this timing, and I encourage you to start counting yours now. Surely God's goodness and mercy will follow you all the days of your life.

- Do not live the rest of your life without faith and hope; at least try. Live your life knowing that all things work together for good to them that love God, to them who are called according to His purpose (see Romans 8:28). The heart of man plans his way, but the Lord establishes his steps. God determines your steps (see Proverbs 16:9).

I discovered that I was hiding my pain, and that was my ministry. But I was afraid. I would frequently hide, suppress, and deny my true feelings. I was afraid of what people would say. I doubted the validity of my emotions, and as a result of this, I suffered silently in pain and anguish. The Word of God reminded me that greater is He that is in me than he that is in the world; He is my God. I earnestly sought His presence in a dry and weary land, and His power and glory fell on me.

It is in my nature to serve God and experience His glory instead of viewing God's glory as a complicated formula. When you are born with the nature of God, it is hard to continue walking, talking, and living like fools. I want you to practice speaking what God says about you now. Declare what God says about you instead of relying on your own gut feelings and low self-esteem.

Your Body is the Temple of the Living God

For by your words you will be justified, and by your words you will be condemned. (Matthew 12:37).

You will also declare a thing, and it will be established for you; so light will shine on your ways. (Job 22:28).

- I am bold, beautiful, and stronger than I can ever imagine.

- I am loved by the one who created me in His image and likeness.
- The grace of God and the fellowship of the Holy Spirit is with me.
- I am confident in the Lord, for He knows my name.
- I am created in God's image and likeness.
- I will fear no evil, for God is with me.
- The Lord is my strength and shield.
- I am no longer an orphan; I belong to God.
- I will not conform to the pattern of this world.
- I am His workmanship, created in Christ Jesus for every good work.

Women must always boost their self–worth and not look to men for validation. Women must feel good about themselves. Women must learn to handle criticism and crises.

Self–Worth

Self-worth is the ground on which you stand. It is the platform of confidence and is unshakable, immovable, unbroken, and unstoppable. Persons with high self-esteem feel confident in their abilities and are able to assert themselves in a healthy manner. Developing healthy self-worth is essential for a fulfilling and satisfying life. People with high self-worth carry a sense of confidence that they will manage whatever comes their way; they don't let shortcomings define their identity. Once self-worth is practiced, self-confidence will be the result. At times, we may not feel the energy of self-worth, but never doubt God's ability or underestimate anyone's potential.

There are times in our lives when everyone has an opinion about our worth, work, and conduct; what is right and what is wrong. Let us look at the account of the woman with the alabaster box. We need to pour out our oil of love from within our alabaster box upon each other and not keep it shut up from each other.

Be Resolute

The Canaanite woman was an outsider, yet she pressed her way to receive her heart's desire. Sometimes it takes a jumpstart to get us out of our comfort zones. Jesus said to her, "Woman, you have great faith." This woman refused to be shut down or discouraged. She did not place an expectation on Christ; she was reminding Jesus of her need through supplication, and we know that tears is a language that God understands. She cried out to God desperately, claiming her legal rights (see Matthew 15:22-28). You too can receive from Jesus, but you must be relentless.

Self-worth is knowing that you are worthy. Self-worth constitutes confidence. The significance of self-confidence is that we learn how to be in a hard place at any given moment in our lives.

It is not by might nor by power that we redeem ourselves, but by the spirit of the Lord (see Zechariah 4:6-9).

Reassurance

- You need to plunder the gates of hell from over your life.
- You are no longer bound by wickedness.
- You are more than a conqueror.
- You are no longer bound by the spirit of lies.
- You are no longer bound by the spirit of drug addiction.

- You are no longer bound by the spirit of prostitution.
- You are no longer bound by the spirit of murder.
- You are no longer bound by the spirit of sexual immorality.
- You are no longer bound by the spirit of witchcraft.
- You are no longer bound by the spirit of demotion and manipulation.
- You are no longer bound by the spirit of rejection.
- You are no longer bound by the spirit of abortion.
- Your shackles are broken.

For with God nothing will be impossible. (Luke 1:37).

The Word of God cannot go void; all God's promises are yes and amen (see 2 Corinthians 1:20).

The Lord, your God, has given you authority to rebuke the works of Satan from over your life (see Luke 10:19).

God made the heaven and earth with His outstretched arms, and nothing is too hard for the Lord (see Jeremiah 32:27). Let every woman walk in the grace, glory, ordinance, and the strength of her God.

Prayer of Dedication

Father, thank You for the gift of eternal life; forgive us of our sins.

Dear Lord, help me to know You personally. I am willing, with Your help, to turn away from sin, bitterness, and hate, in Jesus' mighty name. Amen.

I will not be dumbfounded. I am clothed with power and strength, and I will glorify You without fear.

I have chosen not to live in a pity party but to stay on top of the situation.

I have purposed in my heart not to stop at anything but rather to pursue what is rightfully mine.

On Christ the solid rock I stand, and the gates of hell will not prevail against my standing.

I am the light of the world. He who follows me will not walk in darkness again.

Low self-esteem will not manifest in my life.

The struggles that often come with the fear of making choices will leave my life. Amen.

CHAPTER 2

COPING WITH SINGLE LIFE AND TEMPTATIONS AS A FEMALE CHRISTIAN

Satan's plan is to steal my hands,
keeping me bound from the Lord's command.
Seeking my way
I prayed night and day.
Oh, Lord. Please don't let me lose my way.

I am a part of God's greater plans.
In this life I will shout Jesus over the land.
Deep and wide, He will abide by my side.
The sea is raging,
My soul is smiling.
My sail is torn.
Jesus made it known that I am still His own.

Prayer

Father God, I give You thanks for this opportunity;
For this platform.
I thank You for the readers.
That You, oh Lord.

Purpose in our hearts to read these words.
May our struggles keep us close to Your unchanging, never-failing love.

I thank You, Lord, for this season of a new beginning.
I thank You for every single Christian woman.
Let this word bring change to their lives
and set the foundation for a great Christian walk with Christ. Amen.

I discovered that some people spend hours on social media because they are lonely. Absolutely nothing is wrong with interacting with others through networks, but it is how far you allow your emotions to go and what you share across networks.

Question: How helpful are these connections to your life? Are they more fulfilling than spending quality time developing your purpose?

Purpose

The Lord has purposed in my heart to share with you powerful ways to harness your abilities and stay disconnected from the temptation to dwell on your past.

God's children should rid the church of problems and not add problems to the church. This is a very profound statement. How did I arrive at this statement? Maturity comes with experience. God is alive in us, and to whom much is given, much is expected (see Luke 12:48). The key is to control your thought process.

A strong woman delights in all her ways. Her life depicts modesty, charm, and willpower. The luster of a strong woman is brighter than the evening sunset. Her influence on humanity and creativity is in her nature, and it is very hard to resist by her admirers.

The struggle is real, and so are the urges. Some struggles and urges include but are not limited to the following:

1. The urge for sexual pleasure.
2. The urge for soulmate connections.
3. The urge for material benefits.
4. The urge for financial help-mate.

These are temptations that can bombard the life of a single female Christian.

The questions I want to ask are: How do we as believers deal with new converts and non-Christians when they fall into such temptations? What should a Christian's attitude be towards these people?

We need to remember the days before we received God's approval and His saving grace. The Word of God said by the fruit of the Spirit we can know those who are walking according to the precepts of God (see Psalm 119:11, 133).

In this dispensation, there is a magnitude of lustful tendencies to discriminate and contaminate the body of Christ. To defile the temple of the living God is to be an enemy of Christ. The main reasons for these types of urges are lack and dwelling on a negative past.

There is seemingly a lack of everyday basic or secondary needs. Life causes individuals to challenge many areas of their lives, so several operational activities in one body are going on at the same interval. Some reasons for the failure of so many relationships that end up with one choosing to be single are:

- Compatibility
- Abuse of spouse
- Gender difference

Many single Christians today sought the church as a safe haven. They were not totally and fully committed to God's will and purpose for their lives.

What does it take to stay committed?

If a new believer does not change their friends, ways, motives, and sinful desires, they are bound to hit rock bottom. Love is a must, but relationships are choices. You can love someone, but they don't have to be your friend. Bad company corrupts good character (see 1 Corinthians 15:33). Don't adopt abominable lifestyles.

Single Christian life is hard—no doubt about it—but with Christ in your vessel, you can smile at your storms, even when your life is torn and tattered. You can't constantly make unbelievers your constant intimate companion and think you will escape the peril of darkness.

But seek first the kingdom of God and His righteousness, and all these things shall be added to you. (Matthew 6:33).

Trust God's Word. Call upon Him and He will deliver you.

I had my fair share of living a single life as a Christian. We ought to be mindful of what we pray for. The Word of God reminds us that death and life is the power of the tongue (see Proverbs 18:21). Words are powerful. It is important that we pray God's Word back to Him instead of placing expectations on Him. The mental conditioning required to get everything you see in this world is not mandatory by God.

In the midst of this life, the devil is cunning. He knows us. He knows where we are coming from. He knows everything about us. The devil seeks after you at your weakest point and brings wolves packaged like sheep and parading in the name of the Lord.

If you are a single Christian, be very careful of your choice of relationships. Mistakes have a way of haunting you into eternity. Seek after the things of God, and I bet you will have nothing to lose.

The Elements of Urges

The urge for sexual pleasure: Ask God to open your eyes for the days are evil. Paul wrote about this. He said it is better for you to stay unmarried as he was, but if you cannot control yourself, then it is better to marry than to burn with passion (see 1 Corinthians 7:8-9). Keep yourself pure and acceptable before Christ.

Many people don't have a clear view of God's creation. It was made for us to live in its fullness and not for us to destroy it with sinful lust or anything that is sinful. The sexual aspect of your life needs to be covered in prayer. Sex was created by God. It was meant to be enjoyed. It is not something to be ashamed of as long as it is done in the union of God. Sex is God's gift. This is a fundamental truth. One of the greatest principles is self-discipline.

Sex toys and masturbation are works of the devil. Sexual perversion is the devil's recommendation. When God sees that you are being patient, He will work it out for you. Sex between a man and a woman is one of the greatest gifts given in God's covenant, and it must be done in marriage. The urge for sex is a very strong desire, and the devil will use it to destroy God's purpose for your life.

The urge for soul tie connection: At your weakest moment, you need a shoulder to lean on; someone to converse with at your level; someone to vent to. At this moment, the sound of the wind blowing in your direction and the telephone ringing will undoubtedly appear extremely helpful. The physical man may want to fulfill that void, but the Word of God reminds us that by hiding His Word in our hearts, we will not sin against Him (see Psalm 119:11). God's word to you is that when you pass through the water and fire, you will not be alone (see Isaiah 43:2).

Get involved in something meaningful. Let your life be influential and impactful. Set boundaries—clearly define what you accept. When your emotions go beyond your physical body and your thinking process changes, be reminded that he who is joined to the Lord has become one spirit, mind, and body. The Lord is your refuge and strength when the pressures of single life speak to your body.

The urge for material benefits: Churches need to come in agreement and shut down the power of lack from over the kingdom of God. This is a spirit of disorder and demotion over the lives of our women.

Behold, I will do a new thing, now it shall spring forth; shall you not know it? I will even make a road in the wilderness and rivers in the desert. (Isaiah 43:19).

Is there anything too hard for God?

The urge for a financial help-mate: God promised never to leave or forsake you (see Hebrews 13:5). Your hope, home, and life must be built on nothing else but Christ's blood and His righteousness.

I had my share of the urges for a financial help-mate. I almost let go, but God's mercy kept me. God said He will not withhold anything good from you, and if you ask anything in His name, it will be done *(see Psalm 84:11, Psalm 50:15)*. Call upon Him in your time of need and distress, and He will help you.

Are your urges, needs, wants or lack more important to you than fulfilling God's promises?

You owe it to yourself to be true, committed, courageous, and confident. I have seen God turn it around.

Tithing worked very well for me during my single Christian walk. The Lord reminds us that we should give to Him and He will pour out into us, good measure, pressed down, shaken together, and running over (see Luke 6:38). God knows exactly what we need and want before we ask, but life has a way of bringing us face to face with our lack.

In this world, we classify purpose as taking risks. In the spiritual life, it is in prayer and supplication that we let our request be known to God by reminding Him of His Word. God loves when we pray His Word back to Him.

Set your goals. Pray and express gratitude for the provisions and the people in your life. Envision your long-term goals and pray about them. There may be deadlines or some serious concern that you face, but you must trust yourself. Nothing is wrong with going after greatness, but there are levels on how far one can go. Some people manage the different levels in their lives well, while some crush the very process at the beginning of the transformation. Don't allow money to be your master. Money is one of the cheapest gifts in this life, but we do need it for the smooth running of our daily lives.

Living Free From the Love of Mate

A realistic lifestyle is being content with what you have. Start by believing in yourself that you will walk by faith. Humble yourself in the sight of the Lord, and He will lift you up to gain your independence.

Bold faith is the kind that will empower you through long-term goals. Love is found in works, not words.

CHAPTER 3

THERE IS A PURPOSE IN EVERY TEST

Great is Your mercy towards me, oh Lord—your never-failing love. Lord, we call upon Your Spirit to help us recognize opportunities to stand on Your Word when we go through our tests.

No life is problem-free.
No life gets a free pass.
Problems are no respecter of persons.

Many people face tests on their weakest and darkest days when they are out of options. Tests bring our minds to a place of hope. It is our state of life that gives us the power to unlock some things in our lives; this must be done in a practical way. In other words, it doesn't matter what storm clouds arise; you will not surrender to that pressure but will stand your ground and fight your way to victory during your test.

Tests are real in your life, but God has all the power in His hands to turn your situation around. Tests are marked by loss, misfortune, distress, pain, grief, and sorrow.

Once you stay focused on the Lord, the enemy will not have any road to your life. Your personal direction comes as you develop a relationship with Him. This will help you to weather the storms throughout the test.

Accounts of Great Testing

There are certain Jews whom you have set over the affairs of the province of Babylon: Shadrach, Meshach, and Abed-Nego; these men, O king, have not paid due regard to you. They do not serve your gods or worship the gold image which you have set up. (Daniel 3:12).

Daniel and his colleagues were committed to their faith. The end result was that the king bowed to the Lord of lords and King of all kings. The sinful nature of the king of Babylon was always against the will of God, but there is a purpose in every test, for God knows best.

Nebuchadnezzar spoke, saying, "Blessed be the God of Shadrach, Meshach, and Abed-Nego, who sent His Angel and delivered His servants who trusted in Him, and they have frustrated the king's word, and yielded their bodies, that they should not serve nor worship any god except their own God!" (Daniel 3:28).

Daniel did not ask God why. He was obedient during his test. Daniel decided that he would not defile himself with the king's food. God did not turn up for Daniel until he decided to obey God. God will not reveal Himself to you and not give you a plan of action on how to appropriate the miracle.

God blessed Daniel for being obedient in a pagan country. God stands ready to bless His people when they obey. Daniel stood resolute that he would not defile himself with Satan's kingdom. A test is not necessarily a plot imposed by Satan. God will use untouchable people to reveal Himself to the world.

Though God used Daniel in a mysterious way, he remained humble in exile. Through it all, he gave God the glory. There is no complicated formula for being obedient to God; it just takes consistency.

The three Hebrew Boys lived by what they believed—their loyalty and determination. No power could defeat their purpose because they knew God would not take them where He could not keep them. The purpose of their test was to prove God's divine nature; to stand up for that which is true.

The devil will push you for you to fall, but God will surely cause your enemy to bow down and proclaim, "Blessed be the God of Shadrach, Meshach, and Abednego, who sent His angels and delivered His servants who trusted in Him."

Jonah's Testing

So they picked up Jonah and threw him into the sea, and the sea ceased from its raging. (Jonah 1:15).

So the Lord spoke to the fish, and it vomited Jonah onto dry land. (Jonah 2:10).

The prayer that Jonah prayed became his test and testimony. Every test has a purpose. The Lord prepared a big fish to swallow Jonah. In all his tests, the victory was to glorify God.

Jonah prayed to God, his Father, out of the fish's belly and said, "I cried by reason of mine affliction unto the Lord, and he heard me, out of the belly of hell." (see Jonah 2:2). Jonah emphasized that the Lord is good, gracious, merciful, slow to anger, and of great kindness.

When you set your mind on that place of hope, God can speak to your condition: that problem, sickness, fear, or guilt. Sometimes we believe that our test is a demonic attack. Not always! Our test worketh patience for the glory of the Lord to be manifested in our lives (see James 1:3-4).

We have this hope as an anchor for the soul, firm and secure to represent the presence of God.

Naomi Trusted God

Now it came to pass, in the days when the judges ruled, that there was a famine in the land. And a certain man of Bethlehem, Judah, went to dwell in the country of Moab, he and his wife and his two sons. The name of the man was Elimelech, the name of his wife was Naomi, and the names of his two sons were Mahlon and Chilion—Ephrathites of Bethlehem, Judah. And they went to the country of Moab and remained there. Then Elimelech, Naomi's husband, died; and she was left, and her two sons. Now they took wives of the women of Moab: the name of the one was Orpah, and the name of the other Ruth. And they dwelt there about ten years. Then both Mahlon and Chilion also died; so the woman survived her two sons and her husband. Then she arose with her daughters-in-law that she might return from the country of Moab, for she had heard in the country of Moab that the Lord had visited His people by giving them bread. Therefore she went out from the place where she was, and her two daughters-in-law with her; and they went on the way to return to the land of Judah. (Ruth 1:1-7).

Naomi was anchored by God, and as such, she was steady throughout her storms. Irrespective of what you are going through, God will keep you steadfast. He gave us hope, stability, and assurance that there would be coverage for those who stayed steadfast during the test. Make sure you are under the covering of God before making any decisions about your life. God will bring you back to the place of your past to keep you humble, especially the place where people know of your calamity so they can see the changes in you. Your soul and emotions should be influenced by the power of God. There is a tendency to always be at war with the power of God in our spirit when we go through our testing.

The grace of God's favour was upon Ruth and Naomi during their times of testing. The grace of God's favour is what opens doors no man can shut. Favour is what positions you and puts you into places you have never been before. Favour is what gives you access to Godly rewards.

The grace of God is what guides you when men undermine your potential, push you down, crush your thought process, and belittle your ability to execute your God-given potential and assignments. People might speak badly about you or try to distract you, but no one can dishonour who God favors. The spirit of God's favour will make a difference in your life. It is not by might nor by power but by the Spirit, says the Lord (see Zechariah 4:6). God's grace is sufficient to see you to the end. When you are going through the fire, He will be there. When you are going through the flood, He will be there.

There are responses that we heed during our test in the realm of the spirit that influences our lives immediately. Your mind can program death into your life if you are not careful what you anchor to during your testing. The realm of the spirit is active and alive, and you must access it.

The absence of God's presence during your test will lead you down the path of destruction. God's ways are not ours (see Isaiah 55:8-9). When you know how God speaks, you cannot fall for the devil's trap.

And it came to pass, when he saw her, that he tore his clothes, and said, "Alas, my daughter! You have brought me very low! You are among those who trouble me! For I have given my word to the Lord, and I cannot go back on it." (Judges 11:35).

Some people make demonic vows when they are going through their tests. This activates all kinds of yoke and bondage over their lives. Some even visit the obeah man. Jephthah is a typical example. Death and life is in the power of your tongue, and those who love it will inherit the fruit of it (see Proverbs 18:21). During Jephthah's battle with the Ammon and the Israelites, he made a vow to sacrifice whatever came from his household first. On his return home from the battle, his daughter was the first to come out of his house, so he had to live with regret. So many people are like Jephthah today, declaring careless statements because of the situation and circumstances they find themselves in. For example, "Oh, Lord. If You help me out of this, I will give You one hundred-fold. I will see to it that all those in my house are saved."

Ignorance is no excuse. Many people find themselves in trouble as a result of them venturing into things they have no knowledge of.

You can't fight a war without tests and trials. You must have an anchor, and that anchor is Christ, the solid rock.

The Proof of Maturity During Your Test

Working in a career considered to be a male-dominated one can be hell at times. It is a career that should be strong and unified and essential to command the respect of all. I came up amongst leaders who impeded my progress. My tenor with these respective leaders was crucial. Acting on instructions given, I could not foster an environment where differing views were respected and analysed constructively without resorting to personal attacks, malicious transfers, and tribunal hearings. I was on the verge of quitting my job prematurely, but thank God for my prayer warriors and some good colleagues. We decided that we would not bow to Satan, regardless of the pressures.

I stood up to many years of oppression that came my way in many shapes and forms, especially when it was examination, promotion, and elevation time. After spending considerable time reflecting on my bitter-sweet moments within this noble career, I found myself agreeing with the many sentiments shared by colleagues. There are some rivals who operate as roadblocks to many great women. There are others who seek to build and enhance model-women police officers so that the more mature, educated, and informed this career becomes, the better and greater these women become.

I am still mindful, however, that much more needs to be done to eradicate workplace bullying, character assassinations, rank and file manipulation, transferring officers out of malice, and drawing more attention to the critical issues affecting the members of this noble career.

Her Voice Matters

In the latter part of 2022, I wanted to retire and go into full-time ministry, but I was worried about my many obligations. After thinking long and hard, I began to distance myself from self-doubt and worry, even when it haunted me in a very cursory way. I didn't know how I would make my first move. I had to literally step out in faith and start the process of writing my vision board. Upon completion of my vision board, I commenced vision number one. To God be the glory for all the things He has done. Maturity is a model when we can share our standing respectfully and be respected for it.

Hold fast to your belief and never doubt God. All God's promises are yes and amen (see 2 Corinthians 1:20). He will not go back on His Word. You must walk by faith. Trials and testing come at your weakest moments, but you must never give in to it. There is a phrase that I really like: "Maturity comes with experience, but not many of us handle our experiences well." It is a process of discipline and determination. You must train your mind. What you perceive, you will receive. Your attitude determines your altitude.

Look at the account of Job 42:1-6. There are times when people will make a confession and repent during the test. Even though Job's life was humble and he had no guile in his mouth, he went into redundancy, but he did not surrender to the test. Instead, he turned aside and prayed this prayer: "I know that You can do all things, God, and no purpose of Yours can be aborted and I have uttered what I did not understand and You make it known to me." (see Job 42:3). God showed up for him. God will beautify the meek and add years to their lives (see Psalm 149:4).

Job lived one hundred and forty years to witness his fourth generation. Whatever situation you find yourself in, God can restore you back to Himself.

Hezekiah Wept Bitterly

God hears our prayers, and He sees our tears.

Hezekiah wrote a powerful testimony. He was sick, was restored to life, and sang praises unto God. Whatever your threats are today, seek God wholeheartedly. One angel can destroy a thousand. We may not be able to get to the house of the Lord as Hezekiah did in the midst of his test, but be sure to call upon the name of the Lord. He will spare your soul from perishing.

In the world, we will have many tribulations, but we must be of good courage (see Psalm 31:24). The devil will try to defeat your purpose but don't despair.

Jehoshaphat's Account

Jehoshaphat knew the power of prayer during his time of testing. He understood what it meant to access the spiritual realm. His prayers were not confined to one age group. He engaged even the children in prayer. He needed to rebuild the waste places. He knew he could not fight the battle with his own physical strength; hence, he sought the hands of God (see 1 Kings 15:24).

In his prayer, he acknowledged:

- God's creation
- God's covenant
- God's presence

- God's goodness
- God's position

There is no victory without a test.

What is your test? Will you share your testimony with others so they may see God's goodness?

The test comes in all shapes and forms; some are seasonal, while others are progressive. Therefore, you need to identify the purpose of the test, and align it with the Word of God.

I am persuaded that God will see us through. I have been young and now I am old, yet I have never seen the righteous forsaken or His seed begging bread (see Psalm 37:25).

I have been tested and proven, especially in my career, but God's mercy kept me during the test. What I discovered is that God was preparing me for a greater battle to come. Though I walk through the valley of the shadow of death, I will fear no evil, for the greater one lives inside of me (see Psalm 23:4).

Tests are inevitable and show no partiality to colour, class or creed. There are people in this life who experience nothing but testing. This can escalate into marital problems, suicidal tendencies, and domestic violence if help is not given from a spiritual and physical aspect. Having a mentor or helpmate during and after your testing is potent. Not many women function well in this type of atmosphere. One reason for this is fear of people's opinions. Other people can write your story if you don't understand who God says you are. As you seek to surrender to God, be sober in all your ways. Remember, this is not an event; this is a process. It is like building a relationship with your spouse through dating for a period of time before you make a commitment.

Isaiah said God hid him in the shadows (see Isaiah 49:2). God was preparing Isaiah for what was to come—his right season. Regardless of what the devil is throwing at you right now, God has the final solution to your season.

We can miss our purpose because of fear, which causes us to look in the wrong direction for approval. God created us to function like Him and to carry His nature. The earth groans in earnest expectation for the manifested daughters of God. The devil will push you, but God will raise up a standard against him.

Stop living your life in brokenness and surround yourself with people who display wholesomeness in the life of Christ. Develop a spirit of great expectation, knowing that God will take you from death, misconception, and brokenness. You are not kept by man; you are kept by the power of God.

Here are some scriptures that will boost and recharge your strength during and after your test. I hope you find them beneficial:

- John 1:16
- Ephesians 4:11
- Ephesians 2:9
- 2 Corinthians 12:9
- 1 Corinthians 16:13-14
- Isaiah 40:31
- Romans 12:2
- Romans 8:18

Her Voice Matters

Do not fear, little flock, for it is your Father's good pleasure to give you the kingdom. (Luke 12:32).

CHAPTER 4

PRAYERS CHANGED MY LIFE WHEN UNCERTAINTY SET IN

Commit your ways before the Lord now.

Prayer

Lord, I bless Your holy name. We thank You for Your forgiveness. Thank You, Lord, that we are no longer slaves to sin. Help us to forgive those who hurt us. Help us to crucify the flesh. Lord, thank You that there is no fear in Your love, but Your perfect love cast out all fears, hatred, malice, bitterness, and worry. Thank You for Your grace and favour.

Holy Spirit, remove all doubts and unbelief. Lord, You said in Your Word that whosoever believes in You, rivers of water will flow from within them. Lord, give us living water to drink this day. Help us to testify of Your unmerited love. Yea though I walk through the valley of the shadow of death, I will fear no evil. For Thou art with me: Thy rod and Thy staff they comfort me. Create in me, oh God, a clean heart, and renew a right spirit in me.

Lord, remove all the things that will hinder my walk with You. Lord, Your Word says in Ephesians 4:29, let no corrupt communication proceed out my mouth but only that which is good. Lord, help me to see the good in all those who have hurt me. Amen.

Prayers are treasures, so we are not to take them lightly. Prayer must be at the center of our lives. Don't take for granted the opportunity to have a prayerful life. Prayers open doors that no man can shut, and shut doors that no man can open. If we neglect our prayer lives, doors can be shut up in our lives.

But as for me and my house, we will serve the Lord. (Joshua 24:15b).

The choice is yours. The gates of hell cannot prevail over your life. But if you are disobedient in your walk with God, you will not receive your breakthrough because those doors will be shut. Sin can cause you to miss out on divine opportunities. Therefore, before you pray, commit your ways to God. God can cut off your sin base and place within you the power to abstain, resist, and dismiss bad habits. If you are born of a human being, you are born of sin.

The sinful nature and habits are contagious. How can you resist your sin nature habits? It is important to have your mind renewed by training your flesh so your mind will project rightly to experience the liberty of Christ. Through self-regulation, you will begin to see the habits and their consequences. With guidance and self-examination, we can identify the areas that are broken and are not working properly according to God's divine protocol.

Blockages to Prayers:

- How we connect to God's Word.
- If our speech is always negative.

- If we have no desire to command the things of God.
- If we always believe that delay is dissapointment.
- If we are too emotional in our walk with God.
- If we are too lazy.
- If we don't like challenges.
- If we don't confront our mental stability.
- If we don't pray and listen to God.

We must not see prayer as Plan "B." Living in a camouflaged world is a pattern of behaviour that will expose your fakeness in prayers. Faking prayers can be a hindrance to your breakthrough. The changes in your speech must resurrect life and destroy bad habits.

It is important to cultivate the right habits to break the power of a poor prayer life. A poor prayer life is the consequence of a blockage to prayer. God is progressive; He doesn't count all our excuses. The excuses will make way for lies, which leads to unfruitful prayers.

I acknowledge what habits I need to change. My weakness in making myself so tired from daily routines sometimes shortens my prayer session. Trusting God is what matters to me the most. Trust became the platform for my life.

A testimony of the effectiveness of prayer changed my life for the better when I was made to believe I was fighting with principalities and power in high places that go by the name of cancer. Jesus demonstrated so much action through the manifestation of His power towards me. One cannot serve God without knowing that God is the Creator. He is in control, and those who diligently seek Him will be rewarded.

If you are blessed with the laying of hands, you must be bold enough to speak to that broken body by activating and enforcing life. Make a demand on the kingdom of God that every internal organ must perform according to God's perfect love. Always remember that your body is the temple of God (see 1 Corinthians 6:19). The Word of God is about action (see Matthew 7:12).

It is not God's desire that any of us perish, but for us to have a healthy, righteous, and prosperous life (see 2 Peter 2:9). We must mortify the flesh. Don't compromise; take action and speak with conviction. The source of authority was the very source of Jesus' resurrection.

What is Cancer?

What does it mean when you are told you are a carrier of the big "C"? How does it feel to be living with cancer?

The history of the big" C" stands for conquering death, hell, and the grave.

- **C**onquering death.
- **A**ttacking Satan's kingdom.
- **N**o weapon formed against the kingdom of God shall prosper.
- **C**hrist is risen, and there is power in His blood.
- **E**ternal God is our refuge and everlasting arms.
- **R**ecovery; Refocusing on Christ in a deeper way.

Joan Evans DaCosta

Unveiling My Personal Journey

In 2019, I noticed some changes in my health. I became suspicious, but I trusted God. I felt fearful because my family had a history of cancer. In 1979, I lost my grandfather to cancer. I lost my father on September 22, 2013. On October 12, 2013, while I was burying my father, I lost my sister. On August 25, 2023, my aunt-in-law was buried. My uncle was diagnosed several years ago, but he overcame it and is now reporting miracles, signs, and wonder.

I had an early detection of a breast mass that was suspicious and many results that were inconclusive. This was a time of silence and uncomfortable reports, but often, I let my physical appearance reflect what the Word of God was speaking to my spirit man: "I am the healed of the Lord."

In January 2023, my entire world was shaken by a whirlwind, but there was a stillness within me, knowing that God can do what He says He will do, and therefore, I believe in the report of the Lord.

When I returned for my regular check-up, every specialist said it must be removed quickly. Even though all the results were inconclusive, a brief moment of silence swept over my soul. I remember when the doctor broke the news of my father's diagnosis, and those emotions overshadowed me.

Upon receiving all the results and options, it was time for the surgery in March 2023. No one saw the clouds that were hanging over me because I had worked the night shift up until 11:45 am the next day, just trying to cope with what was ahead of me. Finally, the surgery was done.

Then the news came: "Mrs. DaCosta, please keep your fingers crossed because this is not a good look on your path at all, but I am happy you decided to do the procedure."

I looked the medical officer in the face and said, "Oh, I know whose report I am believing." I even suggested to him that it was a lump of fat. He glimpsed at me with a wide smile and implied that he didn't think so because he had to scrape down very deep. He also suggested that I continue to pray and wish for the best when the final report is ready.

I was still recuperating in April, but I remembered that I had to give an exhortation at an all-night prayer vigil at my church. I looked so dismayed and pale when I got the results from the review visitation. I could hardly walk from the doctor's office, but I pressed my way through the shadows of the evening.

I felt so weak while driving home, and the thoughts of not going to church kept provoking my mind. However, I staggered up the staircase when I got home and was able to shower, make myself a cup of tea, and talk to the Lord. I reminded God of His promise to me that if I served Him wholeheartedly, He would reward me greatly. I remembered vividly how I prayed towards the open heaven that night, and the atmosphere shifted in the heavenly realms. The dawn of a new day came, and I was feeling accomplished.

I became more addicted to prayer than I could ever imagine. I prayed more than I had ever done in my entire life. I slept prayer, ate prayer, woke up with prayer, bath with prayer, and questioned with prayers. There were some moments when I felt despondent. I fought battles no one knew about, but there were many things the

Holy Spirit downloaded in my spirit during the middle of the night when my back was against the wall, one of which was the desire to practice still-faith so I don't put my trust in the situations and circumstances around me, but in the God who is the author and finisher of my life; I choose to only believe in the report of the Lord. To practice still-faith is to listen to God's response as He takes you to another level in your prayer life.

Months passed as I waited for the official results. I held in my hands the keys to shut down the dominion of darkness over my life. I was still a little nervous, but I believed that it was well. In August 2023, I checked my email and, to God be the glory great things He had done, I was cancer-free. There were two significant factors that I still remember: my eldest daughter, Taniel, was so courageous and bold when I broke the news to her. She said, "Mom, you are okay. There is nothing to worry about." She made sure my entire diet was changed. I was looking so skinny, but no one could tell that I was having discomfort because I was working assiduously spiritually and physically. Secondly, my beloved husband had a surgical procedure in London the same day I had my surgery, so we both knew it was spiritual warfare against our lives.

There is no greater tool than the power of praying God's Word back to Him during spiritual attacks, tribulations, and setbacks.

Psalms 91 and 112 begin with the open doors of protection, praise, and breakthrough. God's action in these Psalms brings deliverance. His Word is about liberty. Indeed, we live, move, and have our being in God (see Acts 17:28).

He who dwells in the secret place of the Most High shall abide under the shadow of the Almighty. I will say of the Lord, "He is my refuge and my fortress; my God, in Him I will trust." (Psalm 91:1-2).

He has covered me with His everlasting arms, and I will find safety under His wings. His faithfulness will be my shield at all times. I will not fear what the devil wants to put on me nor the pestilence that walks by night or day. No harm will overtake me; no disaster will come into my life. For God will command His angels concerning my life to guard all my ways. With long life the Lord will satisfy me and show me His great salvation.

Confidence

One thing I have desired of the Lord, that will I seek: that I may dwell in the house of the Lord all the days of my life, to behold the beauty of the Lord, and to inquire in His temple. (Psalm 27:4).

My sheep hear My voice, and I know them, and they follow Me. (John 10:27).

I am healed from doubt and confident in what the Lord says about me. I overturn every meticulous agenda.

'Call to Me, and I will answer you, and show you great and mighty things, which you do not know.' (Jeremiah 33:3).

Courage

Not every step in life is comfortable; it takes courage to keep moving. The assurance I have in the Word of God gave me free course to exercise life truly. God wants me to have confidence, remain steadfast, and hold on to the solid rock in the present time of trouble. Prayer brings courage when there is nothing to be gracious about. My strength boasts in the Lord because He said the sickness that came upon the Egyptians would not come near me (see Exodus 15:26).

The Lord will bless all that I have eaten. He will bless my food and water and satisfy my soul; I will be in good health. The Lord will take away from me all sickness. He promised that no sickness would come near me (see Deuteronomy 7:15).

Commitment

Commitment prepares me for greater impartation. There is a spiritual awakening—a revival—that I am positioned to receive, and that is why I am set apart for God's timing. Commitment and supplication is giving yourself to the Lord, a sacrifice that is holy and acceptable (see 1 Corinthians 6:19). When you devote yourself to God's calling, you have nothing to lose. For to live is Christ, and to die is gain (see Phillipians 1:21). We must remember that our bodies are the temples of the living God. We are anointed for purpose, and this anointing is not to be flaunted nor bragged about. We are carriers of the living water. We are a holy remnant who must be committed to represent the heritage of God's kingdom.

Critical Period

Oh, what do we do in critical periods?

Have you lost that sense of touch with the heavenly Father and are experiencing spiritual warfare? There must be an urgency for the blood of Jesus and the Word of God. When you pray, they both bring healing, restoration, and protection to your lives. Prayer brings restitution; it is not passive reflection but direct communication and praise to God. Prayer helps you to confront yourself and your pain instead of running away from them. Prayer must be your foundation; this is what gives you stability during your critical period. The antidote for a critical period is prayer. Prayer is not getting God to work for you every time you cry, but it is the tool to unlock fear and exercise faith. Many are the plans of a man's heart but it is the Lord's council that will stand.

Immerse yourself in prayer by praying back God's Word to Him. The Word of God is filled with prayers and praise.

To make known to the sons of men His mighty acts, and the glorious majesty of His kingdom. Your kingdom is an everlasting kingdom, and Your dominion endures throughout all generations. (Psalms 145:12-13).

The Lord is trustworthy in all His promises and faithful in all He does.

My mouth shall speak the praise of the Lord, and all flesh shall bless His holy name forever and ever. (Psalms 145:21).

The Lord is gracious and full of compassion, slow to anger, and of great mercy. Great is the Lord and most worthy of praise.

Our Father in heaven, have mercy on our women and grant them peace that will rekindle the fire within them. Give ear, oh Lord, unto my prayer, and attend to the voice of my supplication.

Teach me Your way, O Lord; I will walk in Your truth; Unite my heart to fear Your name. I will praise You, O Lord my God, with all my heart, and I will glorify Your name forevermore. (Psalm 86:11-12).

Oh, magnify the Lord with me, and let us exalt His name together. I sought the Lord, and He heard me, and delivered me from all my fears. (Psalm 34:3-4).

Bless the Lord, O my soul; and all that is within me, bless His holy name! (Psalm 103:1).

My eye also has seen my desire on my enemies; my ears hear my desire on the wicked who rise up against me. (Psalm 92:11).

It is better to trust in the Lord than to put confidence in man. (Psalm 118:8).

Lord, help us to walk circumspectly, not as fools, but be wise in all our ways (see Ephesians 5:15).

God saved us to have a personal relationship with Him through His Word so that we may be sealed until the day of redemption.

Therefore, if anyone is in Christ, he is a new creation; old things have passed away; behold, all things have become new. Now all things are of God, who has reconciled us to Himself through Jesus Christ, and has given us the ministry of reconciliation. (2 Corinthians 5:17-18).

All things are of God, who hath reconciled us to Himself by Jesus Christ and given us the ministry of reconciliation (see 2 Corinthians 5:18).

Every statement made by Paul was based on the Word of God. What more could we ask for? Your identity will be tied to your new birth when you get into a relationship with God. Our duty is to be reconciled to God in whatever we undertake in our work, life, conduct, and ministry.

We must work to repair broken relationships. We must work to maintain the relationship we have with Christ. God desires that we have a personal relationship with Him. The abundant life will never be found in a human being; God made Jesus to be a little lower than angels. He came in the flesh of man to connect with us and to restore us to the kingdom of God. We must be fully persuaded to live this kingdom life.

I am persuaded that God will see me through, and nothing will be able to separate me from the love of God (see Romans 8:38-39).

God has provided us with the Holy Spirit, our Comforter, to teach and lead us into a deeper relationship with Him. God is saddened when we look to sources other than Him.

The Holy Spirit helps us to fix our relationship with Christ. It is our duty to reconcile with God. We fail to recognize our spiritual help, and we tend to disrespect the physical man. How can we then truly appreciate and accept an intimate relationship with God? We must fix this aspect of our lives by repenting, turning from our sinful ways, and seeking Him wholeheartedly.

God wants everyone to be saved and to come to acknowledge the truth (see 1 Timothy 2:4). God, the Father, desires that all people hear and understand the gospel so they have the opportunity for an intimate relationship with Him and believe for eternal life.

In Romans 5:8, Christ demonstrated His unconditional love for us; therefore, the barriers between God and us have been canceled over 2000+ years ago. We, however, have become so cold and callous and lovers of ourselves, even to the point that we forget that God created us to have a kingdom relationship with Him.

And whatsoever you do in word or deed, do it all in the name of the Lord Jesus, giving thanks to God and the Father by him. (see Colossians 3:17 and 1 Peter 5:8).

Set your mind on things above, not on things on the earth. For you died, and your life is hidden with Christ in God. When Christ who is our life appears, then you also will appear with Him in glory. (Colossians 3:2:4).

Let the word of Christ dwell in you richly in all wisdom, teaching and admonishing one another in psalms and hymns and spiritual songs, singing with grace in your hearts to the Lord. And whatever you do in word or deed, do all in the name of the Lord Jesus, giving thanks to God the Father through Him. (Colossians 3:16-17).

The Achievements of Your Prayers

It is possible for us to forget God, even when the Word of God begins to manifest over our lives and destiny. Some people want the glory when it comes, but afterward, all connections with the glory are disconnected.

"Beware that you do not forget the Lord your God by not keeping His commandments, His judgments, and His statutes which I command you today, lest—when you have eaten and are full, and have built beautiful houses and dwell in them; and when your herds

and your flocks multiply, and your silver and your gold are multiplied, and all that you have is multiplied; when your heart is lifted up, and you forget the Lord your God who brought you out of the land of Egypt, from the house of bondage; who led you through that great and terrible wilderness, in which were fiery serpents and scorpions and thirsty land where there was no water; who brought water for you out of the flinty rock; who fed you in the wilderness with manna, which your fathers did not know, that He might humble you and that He might test you, to do you good in the end—then you say in your heart, 'My power and the might of my hand have gained me this wealth.' "And you shall remember the Lord your God, for it is He who gives you power to get wealth, that He may establish His covenant which He swore to your fathers, as it is this day. Then it shall be, if you by any means forget the Lord your God, and follow other gods, and serve them and worship them, I testify against you this day that you shall surely perish. As the nations which the Lord destroys before you, so you shall perish, because you would not be obedient to the voice of the Lord your God. (Deuteronomy 8:11:20).

We tend to think highly of ourselves and are full of pride. Being prideful is to lie to yourself about yourself; it is delusional, a figment of your imagination. God resists the proud but gives grace to the humble (see James 4:6). God doesn't give wealth to us to flaunt it on others but for the manifestation of His kingdom and for us to acknowledge that we can do nothing without the power of God. I have never seen any failure in prayer.

It is unwise to celebrate your own strength and actions. Achievement does not happen by luck or chance. Some of us are a product of our parents and the prayers of our loved ones. If only we could see some of the daily perils and dangers that hover over our lives that we were spared from by the prayers of someone. The greatest achievement in anyone's life is to spend quality time praying.

The real meaning of prayer is not just fighting warfare but submission to God, where you open up to God willingly and freely so He can search and clean the heart and fulfill His promises to you. He wishes above all that you prosper and be in good health (see 3 John 1:2).

Therefore I say to you, whatever things you ask when you pray, believe that you receive them, and you will have them. (Mark 11:24).

If you ask anything in My name, I will do it. (John 14:14).

Prayer should not be a convenient method in a situation but a daily application. It should be a three-course meal, eaten with praise and in expectation of grace and growth with gratitude. These expectations are principles in how we approach God (see Matthew 7:7-12 and Philippians 4:6-7). We are commanded to ask, seek, and knock.

The Lord is my Shepherd, I will not lack. The Lord will supply all my needs (Ask).

I will look to the hills from whence cometh my help. My help comes from the Lord (Seek).

Anyone who knocks, the door will be open to you (Knock).

You cannot fake prayer. God said we should pray back His Word to Him in all circumstances (see Isaiah 62:6). Here are some perfect examples of how I prayed:

— I ask that I may be filled with the knowledge of Your will in all spiritual wisdom and understanding so as to walk in a manner worthy of You, oh Lord, fully pleasing to You, bearing fruit in every good work and increasing in the knowledge of God (see Colossians 1:9-10).

— The God of our Lord Jesus, the Father of glory, may give me the spirit of wisdom and revelation in the knowledge of Him, having the eyes of my heart enlightened that I may know the hope to which He has called me (see Ephesians 1:16-18).

— So that Christ may dwell in my heart through faith that I will be rooted and grounded in love, and to know the love of Christ that surpasses knowledge so that I may be filled with all the fullness of God. Now to Him who is able to do far more abundantly than all that we ask or think, according to the power at work within me, to Him be glory forever and ever. Amen (see Ephesians 3:17-21).

— My soul magnifies the Lord, and my spirit rejoices in God, my saviour. For He has looked on the humble state of His servant, and all generation will call me blessed. For You, oh God, who is mighty, has done great things for me, and holy is Your name. Your mercy is for those who fear You (see Luke 1:46-50).

Prayers help you to be at peace with even your enemy. Fake prayers are dangerous, and this is easily manifested in your words, posture, and attention. Fake prayers are repetitions; they are expressions of self-righteousness. We say one thing with our mouths, but our actions are totally different with people.

Prayers are to be centered on sowing and reaping. The day your prayer life becomes dormant will be the day your focus shifts and you end up with delays or premature manifestations. Spiritual pride is what leads to premature manifestations. Moses warned the Israelites about this type of self-centeredness (see Numbers 10:11-17). The promised land was God's gift to them in fulfilling His promise. It was not because of the good they had done. We can't impress God, but we can easily forget God.

CHAPTER 5

WHAT THE BIBLE SAYS ABOUT DOMESTIC VIOLENCE AGAINST YOUR SPOUSE

In the multitude of my thoughts within me, Thy comfort delights my soul. I wrestled with principalities, rulers of darkness, and hypocritical mockers who sneered at me. When trouble came, my soul did not fear, neither was I dismayed, for the Lord, my God, lifted me out of the struggles and replenished my body on fertile soil built by grace. I will praise His name. In God I will put my trust. In Thee, my heart greatly rejoices, and with thanksgiving, my soul lives.

Set me as a seal upon your heart, as a seal upon your arm; for love is as strong as death, jealousy as cruel as the grave; its flames are flames of fire, a most vehement flame. (Song of Solomon 8:6).

No one can fulfill their purpose unless they are in a relationship with God. A woman is particularly unique because God specially placed her in the garden with Adam. Both genders make life complete. He who finds a wife finds a good thing (see Proverbs 18:22).

So, what comes to your mind when you hear the phrase "Domestic violence?"

Domestic violence is the threatened act of violence against someone. Domestic violence hurts, and it hurts the heart of God. Domestic violence is opposition to God's plan for our lives. God is not pleased with domestic violence, and He has not abandoned the victims and aggressors nor His plan for human relationships. Domestic violence saddens the affairs and plans that God has for our lives, especially when the home turns into a place of pain—doom and gloom.

Abusive behaviour is a sin. It should not be taken for granted. Women were created and fashioned by God to be loved. One of the worst things you can do to tear a relationship apart is to compare your partner with someone else. This is a dangerous practice.

All things were made through Him, and without Him nothing was made that was made. In Him was life, and the life was the light of men. (John 1:3-4).

A wise man fears and departs from evil, but a fool rages and is self-confident. A quick-tempered man acts foolishly, and a man of wicked intentions is hated. (Proverbs 14:16-17).

So then, my beloved brethren, let every man be swift to hear, slow to speak, slow to wrath; for the wrath of man does not produce the righteousness of God. (James 1:19-20).

A couple must seek to complement each other. It is not right to encourage an abusive relationship. Don't allow circumstances beyond your control to be a barrier. Think about the people and relationships you care about. Paul said bad company ruins good manners (see 1 Corinthians 15:33). Whosoever doesn't increase you will eventually decrease you. You need to choose the level in life you want to go. Time wasted cannot be regained. If you spend your time with those who are not worthy, don't complain. Start by becoming selective. Share your love with those who share your heart's desires, dreams, and love for God and family.

A committed heart is a decided heart, and this is what makes a man or woman different from the crowd.

Contributory Factors of Domestic Violence

What does the Bible say about friendship?

The righteous should choose his friends carefully, for the way of the wicked leads them astray. (Proverbs 12:26).

It is important to learn the ways of men.

Make no friendship with an angry man, and with a furious man do not go, lest you learn his ways and set a snare for your soul. (Proverbs 22:24-25).

Many of the common mistakes that are made by women when choosing a partner are linked to struggles with identity crises. I have seen many long-life relationships suffer because of this. The woman or man is not worthy to be someone's wife or husband, but they keep them as their sex slave. A sex slave relationship is very dangerous and can be deadly. I refer to this as an unwise relationship that doesn't bear good fruit.

It is important that your ability and mentality integrates in pursuance of the same common objective, such as your likes and dislikes, your yes and no. You must know who you are. If you don't discover your ability, someone will put a worth on you. Our attitudes are based on fundamental beliefs based on what we were told at an early age. Some attitudes are shaped by societal or environmental factors from within or without the homes. Some spouses are living a lie. Some have been held captive by perceptions of old belief systems, resulting in no growth or development. I want you to start believing in yourself. Attraction is inspiration; therefore, you need to start speaking to your belief system.

Desiring That Someone Special But End Up With The Wrong Person

The person of your choice can determine your eternal destiny. It doesn't matter the age gap, colour, or class. Women are attracted to different things in a relationship. I speak with confidence. I live what I speak. I am attracted to tall, handsome, mature, clean men who love the Lord wholeheartedly.

But seek first the kingdom of God and His righteousness, and all these things shall be added to you. (Matthew 6:33).

If you desire a spouse, seek God with all your heart, and He will give you the desires of your heart. There are many questions surrounding finding the right partner. This has to do with the physical aspect of the human being. It is about that chemical balance and having a keen sense of humour and compatibility. I am not referring to infatuation. I am talking about Godly and wise connection that will last.

Red flags are warning signs that are not always recognizable; therefore, it is important that expectations are realistic in your relationships. Lay all the cards on the table. Share your likes and dislikes. These are vital, even though human nature tends to change frequently.

Weird Types of Love

Some people confuse emotional attraction with love. Women who experience this type of love rarely know anything about the man, and they experience an imaginary shadow. This type of love bypasses getting to know the person, so someone ends up doing stupid things.

Another weird type of love is the quick fix or one-night stand. This is a fatal attraction. Such a woman is guided by speech or presentation. Falling in love with someone you know very little about—except for appearance—is like buying a product based on the label at face value.

After you have suffered a while, the Lord will lift you up (see 1 Peter 5:10).

How battered and torn are you? Hurting people do not wear their wounds on their forehead, but the wounds can pierce the heart to the point where it cannot be repaired.

The scares of domestic violence cause a lot of domestic trauma. Domestic violence is quite frequent among women. The account of Delilah showed that the Philistines used her to destroy Samson's life; she played the role of deception. You must be careful who you invite into your circle. Remember, bad company corrupts good behaviour.

We were created for a purpose; therefore, a man or woman should not be jealous of each other. Both parties need respect. The Word of God declares that it is not His will that any of us should perish (see 2 Peter 3:9).

But may the God of all grace, who called us to His eternal glory by Christ Jesus, after you have suffered a while, perfect, establish, strengthen, and settle you. (1 Peter 5:10).

You may think you are not worthy of living, but it is not too late for reconciliation. God's creative power will work for you. God says we can have it. If we decree a thing according to His will, it will come to pass.

The devil hates good relationships, and he will cause spiritual injuries even to the matrimonial home. He will use anyone to oppress the livelihood in a home. You have the right to control what you receive in your mind. Your mind is the battlefield.

Too many women are victims of domestic violence. They suffer silently, even at the hands of Christian spouses who display egotistical, abusive, narcissistic behaviour. You were not created to live in torture and with a broken heart forever. You need to let go and let God. Stop paying the ultimate price with your life. Stop fixing things on your own. Is there anything too hard for God?

I Am Tested And Proven

I personally cried out to the Lord many years ago, and He heard my supplication. He held me close; I was about to give up at the edge of my breakthrough. I love when a woman knows who she really is. If you open your mouth, God will open doors that no one can shut.

The day I opened up my praise to the open heaven was the day I was ignited with the fire of God to serve Him. I came out of Lodebar and cultivated a new vision. I told myself that I would not let my emotions dictate my actions. I am a woman of strength; I choose strength in every situation that I have been in.

Failure Can Paralyze You

There were times when I was hiding. I was afraid of what other people thought. There is something crippling about the expectations that people have of you. It can be very difficult when you have a tendency to be a people pleaser. It is never too late to become what you want to be.

I want to encourage every victim today to safely step out of the victim role and step into the kingdom of light, regardless of who your abuser might be. God made man in His own image to be in oneness with Him. Mankind is everything to God. He established a covenant for every generation to come; your situation can change.

When you decide to take that bold step of moving away from your wilderness of evil—the abusive and toxic relationship—you will experience a shift in your current state of mind,

Your wilderness can be seasonal; therefore, it is important to pay keen attention to the seasons of your life. In these seasons, there may be dry spells where a lack of communication prevents the flow of information like trust and affirmation, which are vital aspects of any normal life. This can also come in the form of an attack on your progress, family life, workplace, business, and spiritual walk. These seasons sometimes seem endless. Some people even go to the extent of seeking other spiritual help rather than God.

There are justifiable ways of settling an abusive relationship without endangering yourself. Don't neglect the warning signs of domestic violence and disputes. Warning signs are key indicators to detect a toxic relationship. If you are engaged in a toxic relationship that makes you feel helpless, fearful, in despair, and worthless, do not hesitate to get help or advice from an independent professional of your choice. Some of these toxic relationships may demand that you run for your life. Never let anyone try to control and frustrate you to stay in a violent relationship.

There is nothing in the Bible that encourages you to stay in an abusive relationship. There are several erroneous messages about domestic disputes, but there are limited solutions. Some women and men find themselves in crazy-love, and end up psychologically trapped for the rest of their lives. Some of those relationships proved fatal or paraplegic.

Knowledge Is Potent, And Ignorance Will Kill You

From the very foundation, we have always been exposed to domestic violence. It has taken on many meanings from early civilization. Therefore, conflicts and disagreements will arise. Women, especially, are victims of domestic violence.

Domestic violence and disputes are no respecter of persons. We are living in a world where domestic violence and disputes are rated among some of the biggest problems, some of which stem from teenage pregnancy, rape, incest, poor mental health, poverty, low self-esteem, and drug addiction. It is not only these factors at play here, but the bigger picture can be:

1. Outside influence

2. Cultural shifts
3. Dysfunctional family structure
4. Quality of education
5. Civil responsibilities
6. Religious belief/unsaved spouse

Our lives are made up of choices—stay or go, in or out, forward or backward, high or low, increase or decrease, life or death. From my personal experience, and as a mediator and a victim, domestic violence is a wide subject matter. Domestic violence contributes to:

1. Financial abuse
2. Adultery
3. Mental and emotional abuse
4. Inferior complex
5. Inflated male ego

Financial abuse derives from poor planning. There is no cohesiveness in the relationship. Either of the two may be a spendthrift, gambler, alcoholic, or drug addict. Sometimes, the couple might be spending more than they are earning and not exercising proper judgment of their budget. These conditions can hamper the life and aura of the relationship.

Adultery takes place when all common principles and practices around the home have become dormant, and a lack of respect spews from the fountain of love, resulting in either partner starting to stay out late. It could be a possibility that both are playing games of unfaithfulness. The complaint of not feeling satisfied or complete in the relationship intensifies. Couples rarely go out together because nothing feels right anymore—the blame game increases. The food has no taste anymore, simply because either of the partners might be dining elsewhere. Your partner may have become unattractive and carry a different smell than that unique scent you once knew.

You might also notice changes in the undergarments. Every attempt to strike a conversation is nullified, and the excuses are somewhat repetitive. There are comments such as "Do what you want to do. I don't care anymore," "Spend your money, and I will spend mine," "Frankly speaking, I was better off while living on my own."

Mental and emotional abuse: Some partners create epidemic situations in a mental and emotional manner. These do have a direct impact on behaviour. Emotional abuse can be difficult to identify, especially in the upper-class family, pulpit, or political life. The ordinary man and woman will fight it out. Emotional abuse constitutes all the other abuses.

There is no classification on how abuse is executed. It is a likely occurrence in any household. Emotional abuse doesn't just die instantly; this is one of the abuses that can lead to suicide if not treated properly.

I strongly believe that churches should treat emotional abuse with special care. There are people who are saved and sanctified but still hurting in their homes. They are still battling with so much hurt that it causes severe illness in their bodies. There are cases of panic attacks, heart burning, asthma attacks, severe bowel syndrome, and headaches, just to name a few.

Inferiority complex happens when partners compare their worth, insecurities, feelings of inadequacy, and lack of stability. These are contributing factors to the inferiority complex.

Inflated male ego reflects a show off attitude, mostly towards the female. When a man's ego is hurt, he will likely try to get even with that female. An egotistic male finds it hard to apologise. They hardly accept that they are wrong. Men like these are very controlling, abusive, rude, and love to be praised. They take offense to everything. A lot of relationships struggle or fail with men who display this pattern of behaviour.

The Bible says that God hates abuse (see 2 Samuel 22:49). He views it as sinful and unacceptable. He delights in rescuing the oppressed.

He delivers me from my enemies. You also lift me up above those who rise against me; You have delivered me from the violent man. (2 Samuel 22:49).

This verse suggests that God knew and expected that there would be abuse of His people. Our almighty Father—the omnipotent—knows that the hearts of men will become hurtful to each other because of their sinful nature.

If you have found yourself in this type of life, please say this prayer with me:

> *Lord Jesus, let me see who I am. Let us be an agent for change in the lives of others. Open the eyes of my understanding so I may know Your way and seek Your face, in Jesus' mighty name. Amen.*

CHAPTER 6

DISCOVERING YOUR IDENTITY BEHIND THE MASK

My Soul's Anchor

The strings of death and strange voices entangle my life.
I soar above the elements of darkness and regained my sight.
Though a thousand may fall at my right hand and ten thousand at my left, the angel of the Lord will seal me until the day of redemption.
A little one shall become a thousand, and a small one a strong nation.
For I will restore unto you all that the locus worm has eaten away.
I will heal your body, soul, and mind of all that are emotionally crushed.

For years, there have been women who are unable to discover their identity. They remain hidden behind a mask. They struggle with the pressures and issues of life. The mask I am speaking about is sometimes hidden in their personalities, behaviour, status of life, worship, high praise, healthy laughter, broad smiles, great gifts, popularity, social standing, marriages, church leadership, government officials, family life, showers of love, entertainment, and shopping. Women are good at hiding behind a mask during the tough moments of life.

Women hide behind a mask either because they are ashamed of the pain or they are seeking to acquire greater social acceptance. They believe that by wearing a mask, God will alter their faults and shortcomings. You won't be able to hide behind your status and religious mask for the rest of your life. Women who wear a counterfeit and camouflaged personality can cause lifetime damage that is irreversible.

What does it mean to be hiding behind a mask?

You may think that whatever you do behind closed doors is nobody's business. The truth is that a person can be spiritually free and mentally bound by lasciviousness. Lasciviousness is not just expressing a strong desire for sex. According to the Word of God, out of the heart proceed evil thoughts, murders, adulteries, fornications, thefts, false witness, blasphemies, etc. (see Matthew 15:19). These impurities are what some women do when they hide behind a mask.

I have made a covenant with my eyes; why then should I look upon a young woman? (Job 31:1).

The lamp of the body is the eye. If therefore your eye is good, your whole body will be full of light. (Matthew 6:22).

The Lord will expose the secrets that will uncover your mask if you don't transform from that old lifestyle.

A woman's walk is her journey through life. Her directions are focused. The steps she takes every day is defined by a made-up mind. The way she walks affects every aspect of her wellbeing. The truth is, she who trusts in her own heart is a fool. But whosoever walks wisely will be delivered.

Women in this nation are crying out every day in silence, especially women behind prison bars. "Oh, I need to be delivered. I've tried everything, and I am still held captive behind my mask."

Women are always discrete in hiding different aspects of themselves. It is good when a woman can figure out her own true self.

There are two ways a woman can develop this image of herself:

1. **Go through the recovery process. Stop feeding the passion of the flesh by wearing a mask.**

For he who sows to his flesh will of the flesh reap corruption, but he who sows to the Spirit will of the Spirit reap everlasting life. (Galatians 6:8).

2. **Resist the conflict between darkness and light.**

Beloved, I beg you as sojourners and pilgrims, abstain from fleshly lusts which war against the soul, having your conduct honorable among the Gentiles, that when they speak against you as evildoers, they may, by your good works which they observe, glorify God in the day of visitation. (1 Peter 2:11).

Be transformed from the dominion of darkness into the kingdom of light.

The Bible teaches that feeding the passion of flesh will lead to death and destruction (see 1 Peter 2:11). Women who live according to the flesh—hiding behind a mask—will reap the fruit of the flesh. Every dark secret and sin must be revealed, as stated in the Word of God.

For there is nothing covered that will not be revealed, nor hidden that will not be known. (Luke 12:2).

Here is what the blood of Jesus can do:

- The blood of Jesus can cleanse you.
- The blood of Jesus gives life.
- The blood of Jesus can bring forgiveness.
- The blood of Jesus imparts wisdom.
- The blood of Jesus can justify.
- The blood of Jesus brings healing.
- The blood of Jesus overcomes sin.
- The blood of Jesus brings hope.
- The blood of Jesus fortifies you.
- The blood of Jesus gives you confidence.
- The blood of Jesus gives you power.
- The blood of Jesus is what radiates and connects the body to function.

CHAPTER 7

A VIRTUOUS BLACK WOMAN

She is a priceless gem.
She is hard to pretend.
Her beauty radiates the earth.
The sun sets beneath her feet,
Laughing loud is her beautiful white teeth.
Nothing to stop the impression she left on everyone she meets and greets.

W.O.M.A.N.:

- *Warm*
- *Outstanding*
- *Melodious*
- *Adorable*
- *Nice*

Behold, you are a beauty in the eyes of the one you love. Behold, you are beautiful. Your eyes are like doves. Behold, you are beautiful and set apart for the man who will warm your heart.

I am black, but I am comely;
Don't look down on me because I am black.

Her Voice Matters

I am black, but I am not slack in my ways.
I am black, for only a black woman can complete the lot.
I am black. Are you going to accept me or not?

The lifestyle of a virtuous black woman is one that is seemingly expected to set a high standard. The lifestyle of a black virtuous woman must be appreciated. Black women believe in what is right. They fought for equality and to be understood, especially in interracial relationships. I can't imagine what the world would be without black women. I am amazed by the many interracial relationships, especially in the motherland continent.

Our black women are becoming virtuous wives. They thrive in a world that often undermines their God-given potential and intellectual ability, a world that can be so cold and biased against black women. Only the grace of God enables them to maintain their faculties intact.

Black women are special. They produce beautiful children who are pioneers across the diaspora. We find them in many leading roles across the globe. I am elated to see how uncompromising our black women have become. They understand the need for family values rather than just a helpmate or companionship.

We cannot deny the fact that racism has destroyed our black women's lives through slavery. We are still operating in a dysfunctional world that sometimes refuses to see black lives for their worth. We don't need any scientific proof.

A virtuous black woman will ravish the heart, soul, body, and mind of a man. She cultivates and masters the art of self-respect. She knows her worth. She will listen before she speaks. Her mind is very inquisitive. When a woman understands her true self, she will not settle for less than she deserves. She will not allow people's opinions to deter her goals. People will not always like her approach, but that doesn't stop her from standing firm. This woman is not afraid to make decisions when things do not match her values, instructions, or conversations.

When a virtuous black woman is silent, it signals that she is fighting unseen battles and averting certain dangers operating in the spiritual realm. She moves in a direction that gives her something that activates what she desires in life. She will run through troops and leap over walls. The Word of God dwells richly in her. She sets her affection on the things above (see Colossians 3:2-4, 16-17). In her pathway, no evil will befall her, even though they push at her that she might fall. The Word of the Lord gives her protection and direction all day long.

Behold, I will do a new thing, now it shall spring forth; shall you not know it? I will even make a road in the wilderness and rivers in the desert. (Isaiah 43:19).

Jesus repeatedly proclaims that we are powerless without Him (see Matthew 17:14-23). Paul teaches in Romans 8 that our natural minds cannot submit to God nor please Him in our fallen state. We are incapable of even understanding the things of God. The act of God, whereby He makes us alive from spiritual death, is called regeneration. As a black woman, your purpose is not tied to skin colour but to God.

A virtuous black woman learns from her mistakes. She lets go of the past and takes the initiative to acknowledge and be joyful in her success. The sky is her limit, no matter how great or small. She knows the principle of faith is her deed of right and the most powerful ingredient to a fulfilled life.

Black, virtuous women live and age with inevitable grace and vibrancy. She has an attitude for a happier and healthier life that embraces positivity. This doesn't mean she is oblivious to the many social outcasts that come with the struggle to stay positive, but she chooses to focus on building a strong foundation in a world that is still plagued with racism and becoming a victim of racial oppression.

Racial oppression is real and is also operated out of the dominion of darkness, whereby men fail to love each other. Nothing is better than when you love yourself and mind your own business. You will find comfort when you are truly in love with yourself. A powerful mind can handle any difficulty. Life is better when you learn to celebrate who you are. Believe that there is always someone in the world who will value you for who you are.

CHAPTER 8

GOD IS NOT FINISH WITH YOU YET

Chosen And Appointed By God

I will prepare a table before your enemies.
When nations rise against you,
I will shelter you underneath My everlasting arms.

Great are You, Lord.
Your name is excellent in all the earth.
You made us all, both great and small, in Your likeness.
You shaped us to live in the light of this world.
Though a thousand may fall at your right,
and ten thousand at your left.
Don't ponder, and don't wonder.
God is still in control of your breath,
never you walk about and fret.

She is royal!
Her net worth is far beyond rubies, diamonds, and pearls.

But without faith it is impossible to please Him, for he who comes to God must believe that He is, and that He is a rewarder of those who diligently seek Him. (Hebrews 11:6).

Are you having good and bad memories? Here is the antidote for your memories: Memories are to retrace your steps as you go through the stages of life. This is for those who have tasted the extraordinary life-changing seasons of good and bad times. I want you to make a list of your good and bad times and evaluate your now and then. The next step is to pray over them; this is a safe method of accepting who God created you to be.

Giving thanks always for all things to God the Father in the name of our Lord Jesus Christ. (Ephesians 5:20).

Give thanks to the holy One. Give thanks for He has given us life. Give thanks always for all things unto God and His Son, Jesus Christ.

Now to Him who is able to do exceedingly abundantly above all that we ask or think, according to the power that works in us. (Ephesians 3:20).

You are not confined to the struggles of your life. Your life includes everything that God made good about your life. The struggles of life are real, but a relationship with God is a life-changing and rewarding process. It is also the most testing journey a new believer may ever have to walk. This process of life changes bring fear to some women who are totally dependent on a helpmate, while some just go at it alone and trust God for the best to come. Women are superheroines. They were created with this type of nature.

I have seen many women overcome many hurdles and odds that they faced in this life. God gives His hardest battles to His strongest soldiers. God has a word for your midnight seasons, dark patches, and the dark night of your soul.

Women, especially our African native women, usually go the extra mile and try to make ends meet. Some rely wholeheartedly on their credentials, while others rely solely on the promises of God and trusting in His Word to confront that lack and fear. It is okay to maximize your own strength as long as your own strength doesn't interfere with God's timing. When you run ahead of God's timing, you can suffer anxiety and not be able to acknowledge the goodness of God or enjoy His blessings.

Now to Him who is able to do exceedingly abundantly above all that we ask or think, according to the power that works in us. (Ephesians 3:20).

Who do you believe is responsible for your well-being? Yourself or the Lord Jesus Christ? As long as you are relying on your own strength, you will remain vulnerable to people and life challenges.

As for me and my house, we will serve the Lord. I remember days when I had to park my car at the entrance of a main road and hitch a ride to work in order to save money for my children to go to school. I would eat my lunch and take home the meat to make dinner for my children. I scaled down from renting a complete apartment to renting a one-bedroom. I was put to the test in the wilderness for a long while, but through it all, God's mercy kept me. I would cut out buying branded shoes and clothing and save to pay my offering and my one-tenth (tithes) at the end of each month (see Malachi 3:8-12). I was even told by my husband that he admired the way I coordinated my dressing and conducted my affairs, but little did he know how obedient I was to the Lord and the sacrifices I was making. It took him a while after we became husband and wife and started living together. We were having a conversation around the dinner table when he said, "Joan, how were you able to conduct so many affairs that are typically a man's doing? You are doing too much for a woman." I said to him, "I am a committed woman," and burst into laughter with an infectious smile. Then he replied, "Never mind, your Boaz is here. God is a God of timing."

Also, I would pay my first-fruit at the start of the year. This was my obligation, not the church imposing it upon me. The Word of God said people should give willingly, freely, and ungrudgingly (see Deuteronomy 15:10). There were times I felt like God wasn't there for us. My wardrobe needed new clothing. I opened it and began to speak to the wardrobe for new apparel. God showed up in the twinkling of an eye. I am now wearing the best designs from Dubai, England, and Africa. This was when I recognized that my job was not my source. Jesus is my source. Money was not my guarantee. It did not represent my security. Sowing and reaping were my reward. I have no regrets sowing into the kingdom of God. These are the words that kept me: *Your worst has passed, and the best is yet to come.* When you know that God is indeed a faithful God, what you gain will cause no pain. There is no lack to those who truly serve Him. God is able to make all grace abound to you. Ask anything in His name, and it will be given unto you (see John 14:14).

"Thy kingdom come. Thy will be done in the earth" (see Matthew 6:10). This is my mindset, and I challenge all women to make God fulfill all their needs and wants. Who is better able to meet the needs of this present generation? You or God? There is nothing you can do to earn or deserve God's love. He is our provider.

Consider Jesus. Given who Jesus is and what He has done, you must look to Him in the midst of your trials.

Don't procrastinate about your journey. Whenever God shows up for you, go where He leads you. Stop asking:

— What if?
— What will?
— What was?

It is impossible for you to carry on to perfection, relying on your own strength. The Word of God said lean not on your own understanding, but in all thy ways acknowledge Him, and He shall direct your path (see Proverbs 3:5-6).

I pray that the God of our Lord Jesus Christ, the glorious Father, may give you the Spirit of wisdom and revelation so you may know Him better (see Ephesians 1:17). Knowledge is potent, and the devil will cause you to receive faulty and erroneous teachings. Revelation is not stagnant. Revelation is gradually increasing, and Satan is actually increasing his agents to destroy the knowledge of a world that was given to us to have dominion and power in.

Self-discipline is a quality that is won only through practice. According to the book of James, you don't procrastinate and say, "I'll pray about it." Do it without delay.

When you please God by honouring His Word, He will do according to His will and purpose for your life. God's promise begins with Psalms 138:2: *"I will worship toward Your holy temple, and praise Your name for Your lovingkindness and Your truth; For You have magnified Your word above all Your name."* God magnifies His Word above His name. There is absolutely no reason to be insecure. The manifestation of what you prayed for may take some time, but whatever you believe, you will receive.

God's promise: Weeping may endure for a moment, but joy comes in the morning (see Psalm 30:5-7). How about you today? Are you in expectation of this joy? Mary Magdalene absolutely did. She was filled with troubles, but Jesus walked into her life and held her close (see Mark 16:9 and Luke 8:1-3).

There is purpose for every life. It is a joy when you understand that your tomorrow belongs to God and how powerful God created you to be. Every time you are at the edge of your breakthrough, the devil intensifies his plot, but here is **God's promise:** Blessed are the merciful, for they shall obtain mercy (see Matthew 5:7).

It is God who put His Spirit in you and sealed it as a guarantee. Therefore, you no longer have to fear the devil's plots. Genesis 3 makes it clear that the seed of the woman will bruise his head. This was a very prolific statement made by God. Divinity cannot be eroded. God is not slack in His ways; you must know who God is. What He promises will be fulfilled. If the devil has a plot, God has a plan. We are to repose and let the Holy Spirit invade our lives.

Declarations for Women Awaiting Godly Desires

- Lord, let the Word of God begin to operate in my life now.
- I command every darkness blocking my destiny helper to begin to give way now.
- I give myself to You, oh Lord, so that You can openly use me.
- I refuse to watch my life go to waste; I belong to Your kingdom, Lord.
- I compel my life to come under the influence of Your kingdom.

- I compel my dreams and visions to come alive. I carry the fire of God to invade and eradicate every dead potential.
- I have no business with satanic contractions and interactions.
- I break the pattern of family failure, tragedies, immorality, poverty, sickness, backwardness, divorce, and death.
- Open doors now, oh God, that will grant the angels access to my desires.
- I slay the hands of witches and warlocks. I silence the power of Satan's plots.
- Let there be peace in my mind, heart, soul, and body, dear Lord.
- Lord, thank You for answering my prayers.

ABOUT THE AUTHOR

Joan is a Jamaican by birth. She studied technology and supervisory management, among many other courses, at the Institution of Management and Science College and the University of the West Indies. She is a member of the Jamaican Constabulary Force for the past thirty-three years, where she exhibited a vast amount of experience and knowledge in law and police procedure, civil rights, court duties and community policing. She executed her duties with due diligence, honesty, grace, and humility. She has a passion for community development, family values, and the Word of God. She is very instrumental in composing her own poems and songs. She is a great homemaker and a lover of children.

Her experience has allowed her to pursue studies in Christian Ministry at the Bethel Bible College of Jamaica. She is now a graduate and serving in the capacity of an evangelist and elder in the kingdom of God. As the founder of Evangelism Eye Watch, an online ministry that was born out of the vision of Habakkuk 2:2, she uses her time wisely to mentor souls through the spoken, undiluted Word of God.

Her faith and life are guided by spiritual empowerment. God is looking for people who will burn for Him every day, everywhere, every time, and all who come in contact with her must be ignited and energized with the fire of God.

"Where you start in life is not where life will end. God will not take you where He cannot keep you. The worst has passed, and the best is yet to come."

—*Joan Evans DaCosta*

www.ingramcontent.com/pod-product-compliance
Lightning Source LLC
Chambersburg PA
CBHW071224160426
43196CB00012B/2411